EARTH UNDER ATTACK!

TORNADO RIPS UP CITY

Louise and Richard Spilsbury

Gareth Stevens
PUBLISHING

Please visit our website, **www.garethstevens.com**.
For a free color catalog of all our high-quality books,
call toll free 1-800-542-2595 of fax 1-877-542-2596.

Cataloging-in-Publication Data
Names: Spilsbury, Louise. | Spilsbury, Richard.
Title: Tornado rips up city / Louise and Richard Spilsbury.
Description: New York : Gareth Stevens Publishing, 2018. | Series: Earth under attack! |
    Includes index.
Identifiers: ISBN 9781538213117 (pbk.) | ISBN 9781538213131 (library bound) |
    ISBN 9781538213124 (6 pack)
Subjects: LCSH: Tornadoes--Juvenile literature. | Natural disasters--Juvenile literature.
Classification: LCC QC955.2 S67 2018 | DDC 551.55'3--dc23

First Edition

Published in 2018 by
Gareth Stevens Publishing
111 East 14th Street, Suite 349
New York, NY 10003

Copyright © 2018 Gareth Stevens Publishing

Produced for Gareth Stevens by Calcium
Editors: Sarah Eason and Jennifer Sanderson
Designers: Jeni Child and Simon Borrough
Picture researcher: Rachel Blount

Picture credits: Cover: Shutterstock: Melkor3D, Rob Wilson bottom left; Inside: FEMA: Jocelyn Augustino 23, Andrea
Booher 13, 30, 37, Dustie 26, Win Henderson 38–39, William Welch 12; NOAA: VORTEX II 43; Shutterstock: Benjamin B
27, 29, ChameleonsEye 45, Cammie Czuchnicki 17, Designua 11, Dvande 41, Martin Haas 31, Justin Hobson 44, Humphery
34, MarcelClemens 21b, Gino Santa Maria 32, Minerva Studio 9, 15, Mkusweat 16, Photosbyjam 6b, Ernest R. Prim 5,
Dan Ross 6–7t, Benjamin Simeneta 19, Aleksey Stemmer 20–21t, Alexey Stiop 22, Swa182 10, Vchal 4, Vespa 42, Vizual
Studio 33, YexelA 25, You Touch Pix of EuToch 18; Wikimedia Commons: NASA's Aqua Satellite 35, US Navy photo by
Photographer's Mate 3rd Class Ramon Preciado 40.

Printed in China
CPSIA compliance information: Batch #CW18GS:
For further information contact Gareth Stevens, New York, New York at 1-800-542-2595.

CONTENTS

CHAPTER 1
Terrifying Tornadoes 4

CHAPTER 2
The Most Extreme Show on Earth 8

CHAPTER 3
Where Tornadoes Attack 14

CHAPTER 4
Twister Time 20

CHAPTER 5
In a Tornado's Path 28

CHAPTER 6
Living with Tornadoes 36

GLOSSARY 46

FOR MORE INFORMATION 47

INDEX 48

TERRIFYING TORNADOES

Tornadoes are terrifying and violent storms that can leave a trail of destruction and disaster in their wake. A tornado is a fast-spinning, funnel-shaped column of air that can look like a tall, twisted black rope or even a bubbling mass of cloud. Tornadoes are often called twisters because they twist like a spinning top as they move across the land, but apart from the way they move, these whirling thunderstorms are nothing like a harmless child's toy.

A Trail of Destruction

A large tornado can move at high speed, and it can cause havoc as it passes over a city. A tornado funnel's spinning winds can suck up cars and trucks into the air as if it were a vacuum cleaner, and the vehicles were mere lumps of dirt. Tornadoes can suck trains and houses into the sky, carry them along, and then drop them from a great height. As well as ripping buildings from their **foundations**, tornado winds can flatten entire forests and reduce whole cities to rubble.

The trail of death and destruction tornadoes can leave in their wake is sudden and fierce. These fast-moving storms can hit without warning.

Unpredictable Power

What makes tornadoes even scarier is that they are so unpredictable. Some spin for just a few moments, while others can rage across the land for several hours. A tornado might linger over one spot, spinning above the same area of land again and again, and then, suddenly, race off in another direction, without warning. Some tornadoes move across the land in roughly a straight line and in one direction. Others zigzag from side to side, keeping people guessing as to where they might end up next.

EARTH UNDER ATTACK!

As well as twisters, tornadoes are also known as whirlwinds, devil's tails, dust devils, and willy-willies. Their nicknames suggest the destructive and unpredictable nature of these winds.

Big and Small

Each year, more than 2,000 tornadoes happen around the world. Most of these tornadoes are small. They pass by in just a few seconds and cause little or no damage. Many of these weaker, less-severe twisters are not even visible to the human eye, especially if they are obscured by rain or nearby low-hanging clouds. Then there are the larger, more serious tornadoes. These move fast and spin hard, and they can be huge!

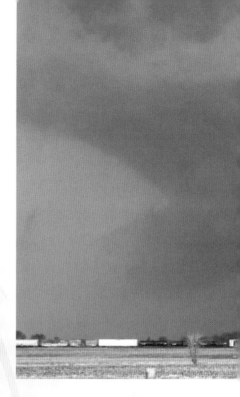

Fast and Furious

The fastest wind speed of the average tornado is about 110 miles per hour (177 km/h) or slower. The average tornado measures around 250 feet (76 m) wide and travels about 1 mile (1.6 km) before it dies out. Some of the fastest and most devastating tornadoes in recorded history have had winds that spun faster than 300 miles per hour (483 km/h), and they have been more than 2 miles (3.2 km) wide. These terrifying tornadoes have left paths of destruction up to 50 miles (80 km) long.

This damage was caused by an EF5 tornado (see opposite) in Maryland in May 2008.

This small tornado hit the town of Fairdale, Illinois, in April 2015.

The Fujita Scale

Tornadoes can be measured using the Fujita scale. Theodore Fujita, who worked at the University of Chicago, invented the Fujita scale in 1971. The Fujita scale links the speed of a tornado's winds to the damage it causes. It ranks tornadoes 1 to 5, depending on the damage they cause. Light to moderate tornadoes are ranked as F0 and F1. These weak tornados may damage signposts and billboards. Considerable to severe tornadoes are F2 or F3, while devastating to incredible tornadoes are numbered F4 or F5. The most violent F5 tornados can rip up cities. Since 2007, an updated Fujita scale, called the Enhanced Fujita Scale, has been in use, in which tornadoes are given EF numbers.

DEADLY DATA

Winds in an EF5 tornado are estimated to be in excess of 200 miles per hour (320 km/h). There have been around 60 F5/EF5 tornadoes in the United States since 1950.

CHAPTER 2

THE MOST EXTREME SHOW ON EARTH

Tornadoes are some of the most extreme forces of nature on our planet. They can blacken the whole skyline and bring savage winds and destructive downpours. Given the violent nature of a tornado, it may seem hard to believe that they start to form in the same way that a gentle rain cloud does!

Clouds to Rain

Heat from the sun's rays warm the air above land. The heat also **evaporates** water from plants, soil, rivers, and lakes. The warm air rises upward because it is lighter than colder air above it, carrying the **water vapor** with it. Cold air sinks into the gaps left by warm air and is warmed itself. This rise of air is called **convection**. High in the sky, the warm air cools, and the water vapor **condenses** into tiny water droplets in a cloud. The cloud builds bigger droplets until they eventually form raindrops.

Thunderstorms

Sometimes, weather conditions provide a lot of moist air in strong **updrafts**. A wedge of cold air forces underneath the cloud, and the cloud expands upward. Big and tall, fluffy, dark clouds form. At the top, the water droplets freeze into ice particles. More ice forms around them, so some particles become hailstones. Powerful winds in the cloud bash ice particles together. This creates particles charged with **static electricity**. Charges grow, until eventually, they create lightning. Thunder is the sound of air expanding when heated up fast by the incredibly high temperatures of lightning. Thunderstorms shoot rain and hail toward Earth in their strong **downdrafts**, with accompanying thunder and lightning.

This supercell thunderstorm is filling the sky over the Great Plains.

A Twister Forms

The biggest thunderstorms are called **supercells**. These ominous anvil-shaped clouds can reach more than 40,000 feet (12,192 m) high. They persist for a long time because of the large amount of warm air feeding their updrafts and strong downdrafts. Sometimes, winds from different directions blow into the supercell and start rotating horizontally in its lower part. The convection power makes it spin even faster and makes a funnel cloud. Then, the **force** of the downdraft stretches the funnel cloud toward Earth. If it touches ground, then a tornado has formed.

DEADLY DATA

Updraft in a supercell can be as fast as a speeding car at 90 miles per hour (145 km/h).

Inside a Tornado

When it touches down, a big tornado is like a devastating vacuum cleaner nozzle. The tornado is connected to the vast supercell, which is like the vacuum cleaner's motor. The suction power is the phenomenal updraft of warm air.

Anatomy of a Tornado

A tornado is shaped like an **elongated**, hollow cone with its tip at ground level. The walls of the cone are fast-spinning clouds. The hollow center of the tornado is called the eye. Remarkably, all the destructive power of a tornado is in its walls. A twister's walls are a hellish place, with lightning bolts and **debris** picked up from the ground spinning past. The eye is a place of calm. Here, the air is usually clear right up through the funnel, the thunderstorm cloud, and even to the blue sky above. A twister shifts position where it hits the ground, so after the eye has passed, the second wall of the tornado arrives with a vengeance.

Lightning can shoot out of the walls of a powerful tornado.

Speed and Duration

The rotating winds in the walls of a tornado can reach remarkable speeds. The weakest have winds around about 100 miles per hour (161 km/h) and these are the most common twisters. The rarest and most powerful twisters have winds blowing three times faster. They blow at the same speed as the fastest trains on Earth. The power of a big tornado can cause the damage you might expect when a speeding train bashes into things. This force is often short-lived. On average, a twister touches down for 5 to 10 minutes, but it can cause a lot of damage in that time.

EARTH UNDER ATTACK!

In 1943, Roy Hall was sheltering in his home when a twister descended and ripped the roof off his house. He looked up and realized he was in the eye of the storm. Roy could see 1,000 feet (305 m) up to the sky above the cloud. The walls of the twister were moving so fast that they were like the slick insides of a glazed pipe. They were glowing blue from lightning in the cloud. The funnel swayed from side to side as it passed over Roy's house, but then, suddenly, all was calm once more.

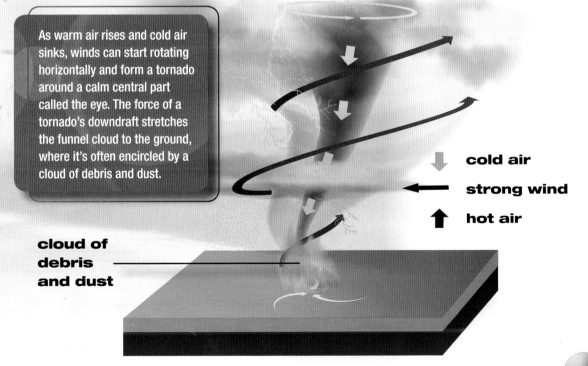

As warm air rises and cold air sinks, winds can start rotating horizontally and form a tornado around a calm central part called the eye. The force of a tornado's downdraft stretches the funnel cloud to the ground, where it's often encircled by a cloud of debris and dust.

cold air

strong wind

hot air

cloud of debris and dust

Disaster Report:
2013, Moore, Oklahoma

Moore is a sleepy suburb south of Oklahoma City with some 55,000 people. Its citizens are used to tornadoes. It is in a part of the country where conditions are often right for twister formation. Most tornadoes form on the open plains away from built-up areas. However, at around 3 p.m. on May 20, 2013, a big twister touched down in Moore.

Colossus

There had been several days of severe thunderstorms in Oklahoma, which is not unusual for that time of year. By May 20, weather forecasters knew conditions were right for a twister, and warnings went out. However, no one could have predicted that a wispy-looking storm cloud would turn into a colossus. This tornado was well over 1 mile (1.6 km) wide when it touched down. The winds in its funnel walls were around 200 miles per hour (322 km/h). A bigger problem was that the Moore twister stayed around for a long time. It stayed on the ground for about 45 minutes, wreaking havoc.

Sniffer dogs help rescue teams to find survivors among damaged homes in Moore, Oklahoma, in 2013.

The EF5 tornado that hit Moore was so strong, it flattened and destroyed buildings over a wide area.

Terrible Twister

The twister scoured a 17 mile (27 km) path, roughly east to west, through Moore, destroying everything in its path. Houses, stores, and offices were reduced to rubble. The wind force battered Plaza Towers Elementary School so hard that it toppled its walls and roof, crushing the children cowering inside. Other schools and the local hospital were badly damaged. The power of this twister flung cars more than 100 yards (91 m).

Aftermath

The lightning was still flickering in the supercell as it disappeared from view, but on the ground, red-and-blue emergency service lights were flashing. Everything was covered with debris and mud picked up by the tornado. Telephone poles and trees were snapped at their bases, and street signs were missing, so it was difficult to recognize the town. It was time to rebuild Moore and the lives of its residents.

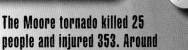

DEADLY DATA

The Moore tornado killed 25 people and injured 353. Around 1,150 houses were flattened.

CHAPTER 3

WHERE TORNADOES ATTACK

Anyone can witness or fall victim to a tornado, wherever they live. Tornadoes can happen almost anywhere on Earth but only if the right weather conditions occur.

Tornadoes Around the World

The United States is unlucky because it has the right conditions for many tornadoes to take place every year. In fact, three-quarters of the world's recorded tornadoes happen there. Two of the highest concentrations of tornadoes outside the United States are Argentina and Bangladesh. In addition to these countries, tornadoes also attack other places, including Australia, China, and India. In European countries, such as the United Kingdom (UK) and Germany, tornado events are rarer. Only about 30 tornadoes are reported in the UK every year. They are generally weaker than twisters in other parts of the world, although they can still cause some serious damage. New Zealand reports about 20 tornadoes each year.

Tornadoes on Water

Although most tornadoes happen inland, far from the sea, there is one type of tornado that happens over water. Waterspouts are an unusual type of tornado that occur only on rivers, lakes, oceans, or other bodies of water. The amazing thing about waterspouts is that they suck up water as well as air. They usually last about 15 minutes and are fairly small, but they can be huge and sometimes high. Although large waterspouts are rare and most are pretty harmless, some waterspouts have seriously damaged boats that have been caught up in the spiraling winds of their funnels out at sea. Waterspouts can also pose a threat to swimmers and even aircraft in their path.

DEADLY DATA

On average, about 1,200 tornadoes hit the United States each year.

Waterspouts are tornadoes that form over the sea, and though often small, they can be spectacular like this one.

Tornado Alley

Tornadoes are so common in one region of the United States that the area has become known as Tornado Alley. Tornado Alley covers the area from central Texas, northward to northern Iowa, and from central Kansas and Nebraska east to western Ohio. On average, this region has up to 70 percent of all the tornadoes that happen in the world in any given year.

Kansas is right in the heart of the area known as Tornado Alley.

Tornado Triggers

The name "Tornado Alley" was first used by US Air Force **meteorologists** Major Ernest J. Fawbush and Captain Robert C. Miller in 1952 when they were studying severe weather in parts of Texas and Oklahoma. The geography and **climate** of this region create ideal conditions for huge thunderstorms. Cold, dry air blowing down from Canada is **deflected** eastward when it hits the Rocky Mountains. When this cold air drifts across the wide, flat area of land known as the Great Plains, it collides with warm, wet air blowing in from the Gulf of Mexico. This collision of warm and cold air masses at angles to each other creates the supercells that can cause tornadoes.

Tornadoes and hurricanes both consist of rotating columns of wind, but they are very different. Tornadoes are smaller than hurricanes and usually start inland. Hurricanes are huge storms that always start over oceans and create havoc when they move over coastal areas.

Fear in Florida

Another area that commonly has tornadoes is Florida. Florida is one of United States' warmest, most **humid** states, so it gets a lot of rain and many thunderstorms. It also gets hurricanes that start on the sea, and when these move ashore, the storms they bring often produce tornadoes. Tornadoes that develop from these storms tend to be less violent than those produced by normal thunderstorms.

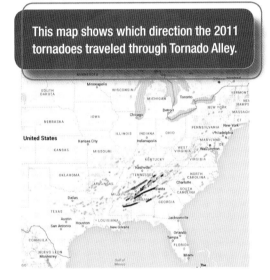

This map shows which direction the 2011 tornadoes traveled through Tornado Alley.

Areas within Tornado Alley, such as South Dakota, have all of the weather conditions needed for supercell storms to develop and for tornadoes to form.

Storm Season

Tornadoes can happen on any day and at any time of the year, but in the United States, the majority of tornadoes happen in spring and summer. Over time, this annual onslaught of twister events has become known as "tornado season."

Tornadoes usually happen in spring and summer because warm air is the fuel that gives them the **energy** to grow and move.

Tornado Season

Tornadoes are rare in winter and mostly occur in the spring and summer months because it is hotter during these months, and this is the time most thunderstorms happen. May and June are usually the peak months for tornadoes, although this varies depending on the region. The peak tornado season for the Southern Plains is May to early June, whereas on the Gulf Coast, tornado season tends to happen earlier during the spring. In the northern plains and upper Midwest regions, tornado season is in June or July. Tornadoes can happen at any time of day or night, but most tornadoes occur later in the day when the ground and the air above it has warmed up from the day's sunshine, between 3 p.m. and 9 p.m.

Tornado Swarms

In tornado season, conditions ripe for tornados persist on and off over days, weeks, and even months. Sometimes, several tornadoes then happen in quick succession. Tornadoes can be deadliest when they happen in groups known as tornado **swarms**. In fact, almost 80 percent of people killed by tornadoes during the years 1972 to 2010 were killed during outbreaks of swarms like these. Interestingly, tornadoes in the United States are increasingly coming in swarms rather than as isolated twisters. Some experts believe **global warming** is causing this (see page 44).

Although most tornadoes happen in spring and summer, fall and winter tornadoes, like this one, do happen.

DEADLY DATA

In May 1999, an enormous swarm of about 70 tornadoes blackened the skies in Tornado Alley for hours at the same time. This mass attack caused 47 deaths and destroyed or damaged more than 2,000 homes.

CHAPTER 4

TWISTER TIME

There are several signs that a twister is approaching. If the funnel of a tornado is not visible, you may see a cloud of debris approaching. This indicates that something even more dangerous is on its way. The sky may change color, sound different, and of course, bring intense storms.

Rumbles in the Sky

If you hear an unusual sound, like the rumble of a train or the roar of a jet engine, and you are nowhere near a railroad or a flight path, watch out! Tornadoes give off continuous rumbling or roaring sounds. These loud noises are caused partly by the speed of the winds, but also by the clashing together of all the debris the tornado is smashing into and hurling around inside it. Unlike thunder, these sounds do not fade. They keep on coming, just as the tornado does.

When the sky becomes dark and fills with ominous-looking storm clouds like this, a tornado might be coming!

Signs in the Sky

Darkening skies that fill with storm clouds and supercells may signal a tornado, but the sky can also sometimes turn green before a twister. There is a lot of hail in the thunderstorms that come with tornadoes, and since this hail is whirled around inside a tornado's spiraling winds, sunlight refracts and bends as it bounces off the hailstones. This reveals the green tint in the **spectrum** of colors that make up light, giving the sky an eerie green glow in places. The heavy showers of thunder, rain, and lightning these thunderstorms bring is bad enough, but the hailstones themselves can be deadly, too. Hailstones the size of golf and tennis balls regularly crash into things at high speeds, causing damage to property, injury, and sometimes, death.

These hailstones are about 2 inches (5 cm) across. The largest recorded hailstone in the United States fell in South Dakota in 2010. It was 7.8 inches (20 cm) wide.

DEADLY DATA

A hailstone the size of a baseball falling at a speed of 100 miles per hour (160 km/h) can cause a lot of damage. In some places, entire herds of animals and fields of crops have been destroyed in minutes by a large hailstorm.

Aerial Attack

The intense winds and powerful updraft suction force of a tornado creates tons of flying, dangerous debris. Most of the damage, destruction, and injury created by tornadoes is caused by objects being thrown around at high speeds. Many of the people killed in a tornado disaster die when objects that are blown through the air hit them.

An EF4 tornado that touched down in Henryville, Indiana, in 2012, tossed around large vehicles, toppled buildings, and killed 12 people.

Making Missiles

Tornadoes break up anything in their path and blast debris in every direction. They can peel off the top layer of sidewalks and throw the jagged pieces through the air like speeding missiles. Even smaller debris, such as tools or computers, can become deadly when tornado winds snatch them into the air and send them flying toward people. People are also killed when power lines drop to the ground and **electrocute** people or start fires when sparks fly off them.

This tree caught some of the flying debris caused by a tornado that killed two people and caused more than $16.5 million in damages in Maryland, in 2001.

Deadly Dust

Some tornadoes smash up so much wood and furniture that witnesses say they can smell the sawdust in the air. Tornadoes also suck up dirt, dust, gravel, and sand, and swirl these pieces around in the air. Although tiny, these particles can cause serious damage when they travel at high speed. They can get in people's eyes, damaging their sight, and can also cause breathing problems when people breathe them into their lungs. When these particles slam into objects, they can scratch against them like sandpaper, and when they fall in rivers and lakes, they can contaminate the water or clog up waterways.

EARTH UNDER ATTACK! Tornadoes do not discriminate about what they pick up as they pass over the countryside or cities. They have been known to lift up groups of animals such as fish, frogs, and tadpoles, carry them away from their ponds, and drop them miles away, so that small creatures unexpectedly fall like rain onto the people below.

City Ripper

Tornadoes are deadly, destructive forces of nature that can cause serious damage wherever they strike. Many wreak their havoc in **rural** areas, plowing up fields of crops and flattening farm buildings. However, tornadoes know no boundaries and can also launch assaults on **urban** areas. For example, in recent years in the United States, tornadoes have hit several large cities. These include Dallas, Miami, Minneapolis, Oklahoma City, Wichita Falls, Houston, Salt Lake City, and St. Louis.

Battering Buildings

We think our modern cities, with their famous skylines and strong buildings, keep us safe from tornadoes. However, when a powerful tornado strikes, it can easily rip up city buildings. The powerful winds can sway or even topple some weaker tall buildings. On the strongest buildings, they can strip off tiles and cave in windows. Tornadoes can blow over fences, power lines, traffic lights, and vehicles, sending debris flying across the blocks. What is more, the heavy rain that often accompanies tornadoes can cause flash flooding on city streets.

Myth and Reality

Many people wrongly believe that tornadoes strike in cities less often. It is true, the chance of a tornado strike in a city's downtown area is less than hitting a farming region because the city covers a smaller area. However, tornadoes can become more likely in cities because of the urban "heat island" effect. This is when the thick concrete and road surface on urban streets stores and releases heat. The warm, dry air builds up over cities. It can then feed its heat energy into and intensify any swirling twister that arrives in the area.

EARTH UNDER ATTACK!

Even EF2 and EF3 tornadoes with 111 mph to 165 mph (176 to 265 km/h) winds can severely damage or destroy properties within seconds.

Warning of an approaching tornado strikes terror into the residents of any town or city, with good reason.

Disaster Report:
2011, Super Outbreak, United States

In 2011, one of the worst-ever outbreaks of tornadoes hit the United States. It was bigger and more devastating than any on record. Over just three days, more than 300 twisters struck 15 southern, eastern, and central US states.

*This was a once-in-a-decade event, when conditions for twister formation extended over thousands of square miles. In part, winds high in the **atmosphere** powered the tornadoes. The result was widespread rotating thunderstorms with hail and an endless sequence of deadly twisters.*

St. John's Hospital in Joplin, Missouri, was devastated when the tornado turned 300 pound (136 kg) parking lot wheel stops into missiles and toppled walls.

During their passage, the Super Outbreak's ferocious twisters reduced sturdy buildings to rubble, cars to mangled metal balls, and even plowed up fields!

Tuscaloosa Falls!

Residents of Tuscaloosa, looked on in disbelief as the biggest tornado of the outbreak ripped a mile-wide path through their homes. This giant twister's winds sped far faster than an express train, topping 260 miles per hour (418 km/h). Most tornadoes strike the ground for a few miles at the most. However, this EF4 beast tracked for hours, covering 300 miles (483 km) across Alabama, destroying all in its path. It ripped branches and bark off trees and destroyed nearly 5,000 buildings.

Missouri Breaks

The twisters disappeared for a few weeks but then returned with a vengeance. An astonishingly destructive EF5 tornado devastated the city of Joplin, Missouri.

In 38 minutes, the Joplin twister killed 158 people, injured 1,000, and turned residential areas to ruin. At full strength, the tornado tossed around cars and homes.

DEADLY DATA

The super outbreak took the lives of 340 people.

CHAPTER 5

IN A TORNADO'S PATH

When a tornado passes over, it can pick up or destroy almost anything in its path and leave behind a telltale trail of destruction. Even so, the land on either side of the tornado may be largely unaffected.

Tornado Damage

Tornado damage can prove a challenge to even the wealthiest and best-equipped nations. In less developed nations or poorer areas of countries, where fewer buildings are constructed to withstand storms, the damage can be appalling. For example, in 1996, tornadoes in Bangladesh, Asia, injured tens of thousands and killed more than 1,000 people because many homes were cheaply built from corrugated steel sheets. The winds transformed these sheets into slashing blades with devastating effects.

Aftermath

After a storm, there will be debris covering roads, backyards, parks, and sidewalks. Trees and tall structures may have been knocked down, and cars may have been blown around. It may be impossible to drive in or out of an area. Broken power lines and gas pipes are critical **hazards** that can electrocute people or start fires or even explosions. There are many other hazards from shattered glass and twisted metal that can cut into broken sewage pipes, **polluting** freshwater supplies.

The tornado that hit Tuscaloosa in 2011 was especially devastating because it touched ground for 300 miles (482 km) across Alabama and Georgia.

DEADLY DATA

Tornadoes cause billions of dollars in damage in the United States every year. According to the Storm Prediction Center, seven of the 10 costliest tornadoes since 1950 have occurred in Tornado Alley. Topping the list is the deadly Joplin, Missouri, tornado of 2011. This EF5 tornado caused an estimated $2.8 billion of damage to the town.

After a Tornado

After a tornado, survivors start to take immediate action. They move from shelters and check on relatives and neighbors, taking care of any hazards. It is important not to enter damaged buildings because they might still collapse. People turn on radios and check cell phones for information about the disaster and instructions on what to do. If trapped, survivors should tap on pipes or whistle to attract attention. They should try to find water to help them survive until they are rescued.

First Responders

Survivors of a tornado disaster need help, and they need it fast. If a tornado strikes in the afternoon, by the evening, temperatures often drop, and the intense rain from supercells may have caused flooding. Hazards are more difficult to avoid in the dark.

Rescue teams search house to house for survivors in tornado-devastated Moore, Oklahoma, in 2013.

Rescue Teams

Rescue teams arrive by road if routes are clear, or on foot or by helicopter. Health workers treat injuries that typically include broken limbs, cuts from debris, and eye problems from swirling dust. They also treat survivors for shock because they may have lost everything or witnessed horrifying injuries. Rescuers including the armed forces, fire services, the National Guard, and volunteers start the search for the missing. They may use sniffer dogs that are trained to smell humans hidden beneath deep rubble. Rescue teams use anything from their gloved hands and spades to cranes, diggers, and chain saws to reach trapped survivors.

Emergency workers are usually the first to arrive after a tornado hits.

Safe Environment

One priority after a tornado is removing the hazards from the disaster zone. Rescue teams may disconnect or mend broken power lines and water and gas pipes. They sweep up broken glass, nails, and other sharp objects. It is vital that emergency workers protect themselves during this work, for example, by wearing safety boots to protect their feet and masks to avoid breathing in too much dust.

Survivors often have no homes to return to. So disaster response teams may use local schools or other buildings to temporarily house survivors. They set up beds and canteens there, so that families can sleep and eat. In situations where there are few buildings standing, rescuers may set up tent camps for survivors.

EARTH UNDER ATTACK!

The scents that sniffer dogs can detect are human skin cells. These naturally wear off our bodies by the thousands in our sweat and the gases we breathe out. Dogs sniff the air to detect these traces of people. They can crawl into tiny spaces that rescuers cannot and climb over rubble that would collapse under a heavy human. Sniffer dogs stay still and bark at any place where they have located a hidden survivor.

Rebuilding Lives

After the injured are treated and the survivors tended to, it is time to turn the disaster zone into a place to live once more. There is no quick fix to this: It is a process that takes time and involves many people.

Shifting Debris

Using bulldozers and trucks, builders and armed forces work to clear the debris. Some waste that is more hazardous needs to be handled very carefully. For example, fiberglass is made from tiny fibers that can cause illnesses when breathed in; so to remain safe, those dealing with it must wear breathing masks. People return to their properties to salvage anything they can, from personal mementos, such as family photographs, to tools and clothing.

Reconstruction

The foundations of buildings may be all that remains intact after a twister. Engineers check the structural safety of these and any damaged buildings before any rebuilding takes place. Once this is done, new buildings are planned. Building materials and professional builder salaries are expensive, so at many tornado strike sites, at least some of the rebuilding is up to volunteers.

People want to help but may not have enough skills or experience to rebuild to high standards. Communities sometimes get help from outside organizations such as the St. Bernard Project, which specializes in construction after natural disasters. These help to plan and coordinate work, source cheap materials, and use volunteers' skills in the most effective way. Gradually, when communities work together, homes and lives are rebuilt.

A woman cleans up after tornadoes hit the St. Louis area in April 2011.

Heavy equipment often has to be used to clean up and clear all of the debris and damage left by a powerful tornado.

Sometimes, disasters are too great for local or state governments to cope with. Then, leaders declare a "state of emergency," and large agencies get involved. These include charities such as the Red Cross and international agencies. In the United States, the government mobilizes the Federal Emergency Management Agency (FEMA) after big disasters. FEMA coordinates first response, clean up, and rebuilding, as well as security, to prevent people from **looting** disaster sites.

Disaster Report:
2016, Jiangsu, China

*The skies turned as dark as night, and residents of Yancheng city, in Jiangsu Province, eastern China, waited for the rains in the early afternoon of June 23, 2016. This part of early summer is when heavy rain normally falls, but in 2016, around the country, there had been heavier rain than usual. Flooding from thunderstorms had already **displaced** nearly 200,000 people in the south of the country, where swollen rivers burst their banks.*

Transportation is difficult with flooding. When floodwater fills people's homes, it destroys their belongings and forces them to leave their homes.

EARTH UNDER ATTACK!

Rains heavier than usual were the result of a vast mass of cooler than normal air from the north, clashing with unusually warm air from the south. The undercutting of the cold air pushed cloud tops unusually high into the atmosphere. These were textbook conditions, not only for supercells but also for tornadoes.

This **satellite** image shows the thunderstorm that spawned the terrifying tornado that hit Jiangsu in China, in 2016.

Apocalypse

However, in Yancheng, people sheltering in their homes were terribly surprised when a tornado struck. Witnesses estimated the winds at just 80 miles per hour (129 km/h), yet later analysis by meteorologists took a different view. The damage was consistent with an EF5 event, with winds twice this speed. These winds and the violent updraft and suction produced devastating destruction. Power pylons buckled. Trees were uprooted, and cars were plucked from roads and thrown high into the sky. Roofs were blown off, and walls and windows caved in. Dust, straw, and broken glass from the ground, with hailstones from the supercell clouds, shot like bullets through the air.

Aftermath and Response

The Jiangsu tornado injured around 800 people and killed 98. Chinese authorities said it was the worst tornado to hit the country in 50 years, and the government declared a national emergency. It was clear that people did not know what to do in the event of a tornado, and there was a lack of emergency response teams. The Chinese president called for an all-out rescue effort, and hundreds of rescuers were dispatched to Yancheng in particular. By the time the rescuers arrived, they were too late to save some of the trapped survivors. Yet they cleared away dead bodies, carried the injured to ambulances, and set up temporary shelters for the survivors.

CHAPTER 6

LIVING WITH TORNADOES

Many people live in areas where tornadoes are quite common, such as Tornado Alley. There is nothing that they can really do to prevent tornadoes from hitting their homes and towns in the future. Instead, they make plans and preparations to reduce the risks that tornadoes cause them and their property.

Take Shelter

The first thing to think about is making or choosing a safe place to take shelter during a tornado. Many people build safe rooms or storm shelters. These may be in basements or built underground. The walls are built with **reinforced** concrete or brick. They have no windows, and they have a heavy concrete floor and roof that cannot be pulled off or damaged by a tornado's winds or smashed by large debris dropped by a tornado. It is impossible to build a tornado-proof home to live in all the time: It would have to have windows that could withstand a refrigerator flying through the air at 200 miles per hour (322 km/h). Instead, people make sure they are safe in their storm shelter, and they hope their homes do not suffer too much damage while they are in there.

Safe rooms or shelters built below ground provide people with the greatest protection.

Evacuation Plans

Families also draw up an **evacuation** plan and gather equipment to help them survive when there is a tornado warning. They should know where the shelters, or safe places to shelter, are near their homes, schools, and places of work. They should also buy a basic emergency supply kit and keep it handy. This should contain useful items, such as water, dried and canned food, battery-powered radio and flashlight, spare batteries, a first-aid kit, and a whistle to signal for help.

EARTH UNDER ATTACK!

The average forward speed of a tornado is 30 miles per hour (48 km/h), but this may reach 70 miles per hour (113 km/h). Some people try to outdrive tornadoes in their cars, but this is inadvisable. If a tornado passes over a car, it can toss or roll the vehicle about, over and over again, and even pick it up and hurl it into nearby buildings or trees.

Early Warning

During tornado season, it pays to learn what danger signs to watch out for. Indications that a tornado might be approaching include a dark, often greenish sky, big hailstones falling, a large, dark, low-lying cloud, a loud roaring sound, or an approaching storm. Most communities in tornado-prone regions also have warning systems in place to advise people about what to do and to warn them if a tornado is imminent.

Tornado sirens like this are fixed to central buildings in a town or city, so that their warning blasts can be heard all around.

Tornado Watch

In the United States, the National Weather Service issues two types of warnings. The first is a tornado watch. When a tornado watch is announced, it means the weather conditions make tornadoes more likely. It does not mean that anyone has seen a tornado coming or that one will definitely happen. It means that tornadoes are possible, and people should remain alert for approaching storms. They should watch the sky for danger signs and stay tuned to their radios or TVs for more information. They should also make sure friends and family know that there is a risk of tornadoes in the area. Some people also board up their windows, trim back branches that could be snapped off and cause damage, or strap roof tiles down, so that they will not blow off so easily.

Tornado Warning

The second warning is a tornado warning. This means a tornado has been spotted or that meteorologists have identified conditions that could easily set off a tornado. It is now time for people to go straight to a shelter. There is no time to do anything else. If no storm shelter or safe room is available, people should head for a basement or a room on a lower-ground floor that has no windows. People should leave mobile homes immediately, since tornadoes can easily pick these up or completely flatten them.

DEADLY DATA

Across the United States, tornadoes cause about 80 deaths and more than 1,500 injuries in an average year. Approximately 45 percent of these deaths were people living in mobile homes.

Know Your Twister

Twisters are so unpredictable that it is impossible to ensure that people are never in their paths. However, meteorologists study tornadoes in order to understand their paths, forces, and formation conditions, so they can understand them better. They do this with the hope of being able to give people more warning about when and where twisters might occur.

Weather Technology

Weather balloons collect data from inside thunderstorms where it is too dangerous for research aircraft to fly.

To create the best **forecasts** they can, meteorologists use a variety of technology to gather information, from weather balloons to satellites in space. Weather balloons float into thunderstorms where the **sensors** attached to them measure data about conditions inside the storm, such as temperature, air pressure, and wind speed. Meteorologists combine these measurements with information from other equipment, such as satellites that sense moisture in the atmosphere, and images of the locations, shape, and size of clouds. They use computers to analyze this information, along with weather reports, to produce **computer models** of ways a storm might behave. All these things can help create a forecast about where and when a storm will strike and how bad it will be.

Radar domes like this send out radio waves. They calculate the distance to the target by recording the time it takes those waves to hit the target and return to the antenna.

Weather Radar

Many tornadoes are also detected using weather radar. Radar beams bounce off droplets of moisture inside a cloud. Machines that receive the reflected signal can tell the density of moisture, snow, hail, or dust in the storm system by how strong the signal is. The reflected signals also reveal what direction the wind is moving and if the air is spinning. If it is, that is a sign that a tornado may form.

EARTH UNDER ATTACK! ▶

Sometimes, people mistake a gustnado for a tornado. Gustnadoes are small, weak gusts of whirling winds that form from the front of thunderstorms. They often have a spinning dust cloud at ground level, like tornadoes. They can do minor damage, such as breaking windows and tree branches. However, unlike a tornado, the rotating column of air in a gustnado is not connected to the base of a cloud.

Storm Chasers

When most people see dark clouds looming and a major storm approaching, they flee in the opposite direction. There are some people, however, who do not follow this natural impulse. They deliberately track and follow dangerous tornadoes, usually in specially adapted vans or trucks, but sometimes by airplane or helicopter.

On the Alert

Storm chasers go to tornado-prone areas, such as Tornado Alley in the central part of the United States. They wait in vans with weather monitoring equipment and keenly study the radar data flashing on computer screens in their vehicles. They listen closely to radio updates about storms. As soon as they see or hear evidence that a big storm is brewing, they head toward it, all the while watching out for that distinctive lowering of the cloud base that can seed a tornado.

Storm chasers report their tornado sightings to weather forecasters to help them predict where the tornado will go next.

Storm chasers' vehicles are reinforced to keep the occupants safe. They carry all the equipment they need to monitor the storms overhead.

Chasing Equipment

Many of these daring storm chasers put their lives at risk for the fun and excitement of witnessing a giant twister. Other storm chasers are meteorologists or amateur scientists who set out to gather information, photos, and videos of these amazing weather events to help them in their studies. They often have special radar equipment that can be mounted to the back of a truck, and their trucks are heavily reinforced so that it is harder for a tornado to lift them. They have body panels that can lower to ground level to stop tornado winds from getting underneath the truck. The trucks may also have jacks that can be lowered to keep vehicles stable.

DEADLY DATA

The Tornado Intercept Vehicle (TIV) is a specially designed storm-chasing vehicle that weighs 8 tons (7.2 metric tons). It has special plastic windows in a turret that can turn, so the crew inside can film in any direction. Its body and floor are made from steel.

Future Tornadoes

Tornadoes are awesome forces of nature that will always make news headlines. However, it is bad news that there could be changing patterns and numbers of tornadoes in the future. The reason is global warming.

Experts believe we could see more tornadoes in the future.

Changing Atmosphere

Most scientists agree that Earth's atmosphere is getting warmer. This is happening because human activities, such as burning fuels in power plants, are creating more gases, such as carbon dioxide, which stay in the atmosphere. The gases store heat from the sun, so the planet gets very gradually warmer. Global warming is changing weather patterns around the world. For example, formerly wet areas are becoming drier, and there are increasing numbers of extreme weather events, such as tornadoes. Tornadoes form where there is very warm, moist air clashing with colder air, so it makes sense that changing weather might cause tornadoes in places that have not experienced them before. Global warming may also increase the severity of tornadoes in places that do have them.

Improved Warnings

In the future, scientists will fly drones, or flying robots, into supercells to get better data. Drones have the advantage over storm-tracking humans in that they can take flight cheaply and with no risk to pilots. The tornado drones are tough machines that will fly fast through the twister wall and then get sucked up on the updraft. They have sensors to measure forces, wind speeds, temperatures, and other data from the storms. Even if the drones are destroyed, the data collection boxes they carry are bulletproof, and can be salvaged after the storm by scientists, a little like black boxes from crashed airplanes.

Around 70 percent of tornado warnings prove to be false alarms, so using equipment such as drones should help make it possible to predict tornadoes hours in advance. It might not stop the damage, but it will enable many more people to take proper shelter or even escape strike zones.

Although there may be more tornadoes in the future, people are getting better at predicting them, preparing for them, and helping victims after one strikes.

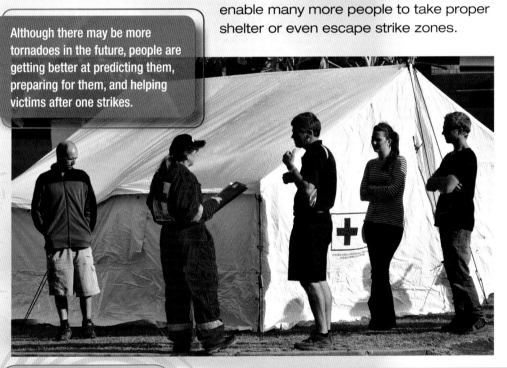

DEADLY DATA

In the 1960s, people got just a few seconds warning before tornado strikes. Today, warnings can give people around 15 minutes. The reason is that scientists have more accurate data from weather balloons, satellite sensors, and storm chasers.

GLOSSARY

atmosphere a blanket of gases around a planet

climate the usual pattern of weather that happens in a place

computer models computer program that uses data, math, and computer instructions to predict events in the real world

condenses changes from a gas to a liquid

convection when the warmer parts in a gas or liquid move up and the colder parts move down

debris fragments left after something has been destroyed

deflected made to change direction

displaced forced to leave home, for example, because of a natural disaster

downdrafts downward currents or drafts of air

electrocute when electricity injures or kills someone as it passes through their body

elongated stretched out

energy the ability to do work

evacuation moving people from a dangerous to a safe place

evaporates turns from a liquid into a vapor or gas

force a push or pull that can change the way things move

forecasts predictions about the weather

foundations weight-bearing parts of a building below ground level

funnel-shaped something that is long and wider at the top and skinny on the bottom, like an ice cream cone

global warming changes in the world's weather patterns caused by human activity

hazards dangers or risks

humid describes something with a lot of moisture in the air

looting stealing from other people's property, especially after a disaster

meteorologists scientists who study Earth's atmosphere and weather

polluting damaging or harming the air, water, soil, or other parts of the environment

radar a way of finding the position of an object by bouncing a radio wave off it and analyzing the reflected wave

reinforced strengthened

rural to do with the countryside

satellites man-made objects in orbit above Earth that can take images of Earth's atmosphere

sensors devices that detect and measure something, such as amounts of a particular gas in the air

sniffer dogs dogs trained to use their sense of smell to find things

spectrum a range or band of colors

static electricity electric charge that has built up on an object

supercells unusual thunderstorms with a deep, rotating updraft

swarms large groups of things moving together

updrafts warm columns of air rising in a cloud

urban to do with cities or towns

water vapor water in the form of a gas

FOR MORE INFORMATION

BOOKS

Baker, John R. *The World's Worst Tornadoes*. North Mankato, MN: Capstone Press, 2016.

Bowman, Chris. *Survive a Tornado* (Survival Zone). Hopkins, MN: Bellwether Media, 2016.

Fradin, Judith and Dennis Fradin. *Tornado!: The Story Behind These Twisting, Turning, Spinning, and Spiraling Storms* (National Geographic Kids). Washington, DC: National Geographic, 2011.

Tarshis, Lauren. *Tornado Terror* (I Survived True Stories). New York, NY: Scholastic Press, 2017.

WEBSITES

Learn more about how to prepare for and survive twisters at:
www.ready.gov/tornadoes

Want to know more about how tornadoes work? Go to:
science.howstuffworks.com/nature/climate-weather/storms/tornado.htm

View the excitement of a storm chase, and witness the power of twisters at:
www.discovery.com/tv-shows/storm-chasers/videos/grand-slam-intercept

Witness the astonishing tornado super outbreak swarm of 2011 in Tornado Alley at:
www.youtube.com/watch?v=JtJX903Sxt4

If you have any unanswered questions about tornadoes, why not visit this website for some answers?
www.spc.noaa.gov/faq/tornado

Publisher's note to educators and parents: Our editors have carefully reviewed these websites to ensure that they are suitable for students. Many websites change frequently, however, and we cannot guarantee that a site's future contents will continue to meet our high standards of quality and educational value. Be advised that students should be closely supervised whenever they access the Internet.

INDEX

Argentina 14

Australia 14

Bangladesh 14, 28

Canada 16

China 14, 34–35

climate 16

cloud 4, 6, 8, 9, 10, 11, 12, 20, 34, 35, 38, 40, 41, 42

convection 8, 9

danger signs 20, 38, 39, 41

devil's tails 5

downdrafts 8, 9, 11

drones 45

dust 11, 23, 30, 31, 35, 41

dust devils 5

emergency supply kit 37

Enhanced Fujita Scale 7

evacuation 37

eye (of tornado) 10, 11

first responders 30–31

flooding 24, 30, 34

forecasters 12, 40, 42

Fujita scale 7

funnels 4, 9, 10, 11, 12, 14, 20

Germany 14

global warming 19, 44

hail and hailstones 8, 20–21, 26, 35, 38, 41

Henryville, Indiana 22

India 14

Joplin, Missouri 26, 27, 29

lightning 8, 10, 11, 13, 20

Moore, Oklahoma 12–13, 30

New Zealand 14

radar 41, 42, 43

rain 6, 8, 17, 20, 24, 30, 34

raining animals 23

rebuilding 13, 32–33

safe rooms 36, 37, 39

sniffer dogs 12, 30, 31

St. Bernard Project 32

static electricity 8

storm chasers 42–43, 45

storm shelters 36, 37, 39

supercells 9, 10, 13, 16, 20, 30, 34, 35, 45

swarms 19

thunder and thunderstorms 4, 8, 9, 10, 12, 16, 17, 18, 20, 26, 34, 35, 40, 41

Tornado Alley 16–17, 19, 29, 36, 42

tornado season 18–19, 38

Tuscaloosa, Alabama 27, 29

twisters 4, 5, 6, 9, 10, 11, 12, 13, 14, 18, 19, 20, 24, 26, 27, 32, 40, 43, 45

United Kingdom 14

United States 7, 12–13, 14, 15, 16, 17, 18, 19, 21, 24, 26, 27, 29, 33, 39, 42

updrafts 8, 9, 10, 22, 35, 45

walls (of a tornado) 10, 11, 12, 45

warnings 5, 12, 25, 37, 38–39, 40, 45

water vapor 8

waterspouts 14, 15

weather 8, 12, 14, 16, 39, 40–41, 42, 43, 44, 45

weather balloons 40, 45

whirlwinds 5

willy-willies 5

wind 4, 5, 6, 7, 8, 9, 11, 12, 13, 14, 17, 20, 22, 24, 26, 27, 28, 35, 36, 40, 41, 43, 45